Make It 100!

Joanne Mattern

ROURKE PUBLISHING
www.rourkepublishing.com

www.rourkepublishing.com

PHOTO CREDITS: Cover: © Christophe Testi, Dan Breckwoldt, Riderofthestorm, Elaromy; Title Page: © Marco Martins; Page 3: © Dmitriy Shironosov; Page 4, 7: © subjug; Page 5: © Daniel Laflor; Page 6: © Joshua Hodge Photography; Page 8: © Dmitry Kalinovsky; Page 9: © Hongqi Zhang; Page 10, 11: © juicybits, Lisa Thornberg, Beata Becla; Page 12, 13, 15, 16, 17: © oleksiy; Page 14: © Joshua Hodge Photography; Page 18: © nito500; Page 19: © Javier Pazo, Lee Daniels; Page 20, 21: © Vasko Miokovic; Page 22: © juicybits, Beata Becla, subjug; Page 23: © oleksiy, Vasko Miokovic;

Edited by Luana Mitten

Cover and Interior design by Teri Intzegian

Library of Congress Cataloging-in-Publication Data

Mattern, Joanne
  Make It 100! / Joanne Mattern.
    p. cm. -- (Little World Math)
  Includes bibliographical references and index.
  ISBN 978-1-61741-765-8 (hard cover) (alk. paper)
  ISBN 978-1-61741-967-6 (soft cover)
  Library of Congress Control Number: 2011924812

Rourke Publishing
Printed in the United States of America, North
Mankato, Minnesota
060711
060711CL

www.rourkepublishing.com - rourke@rourkepublishing.com
Post Office Box 643328 Vero Beach, Florida 32964

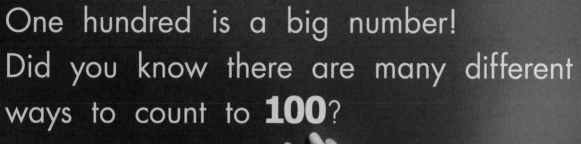

One hundred is a big number!
Did you know there are many different
ways to count to **100**?

You can count to 100 by 1's.
Let's count!

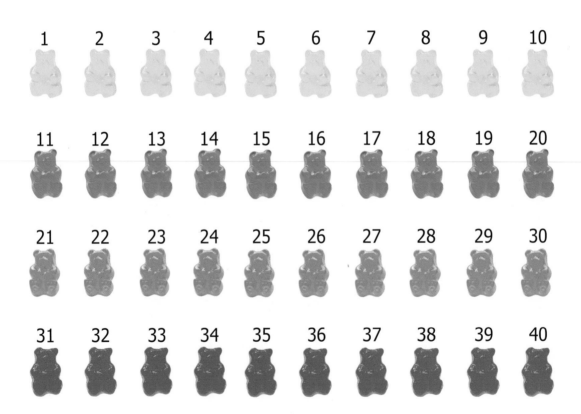

Keep counting!

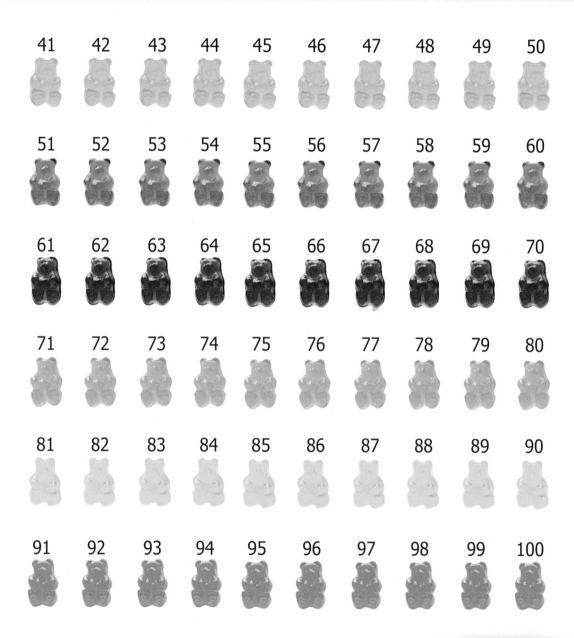

You can count to 100 by 2's.
Let's count!

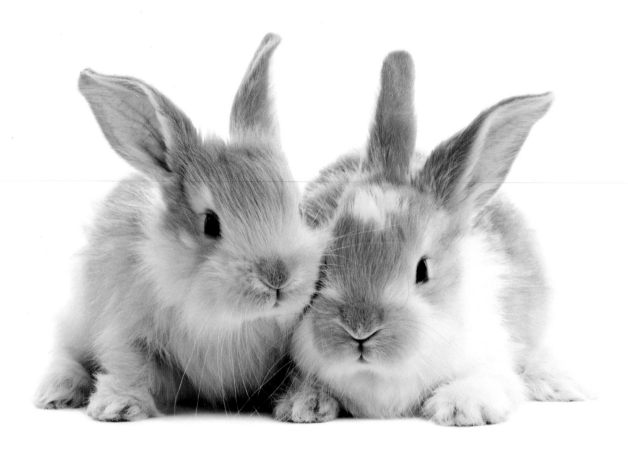

2, 4, 6,
8, 10...

2   4   6   8   10

12   14   16   18   20

Keep counting!

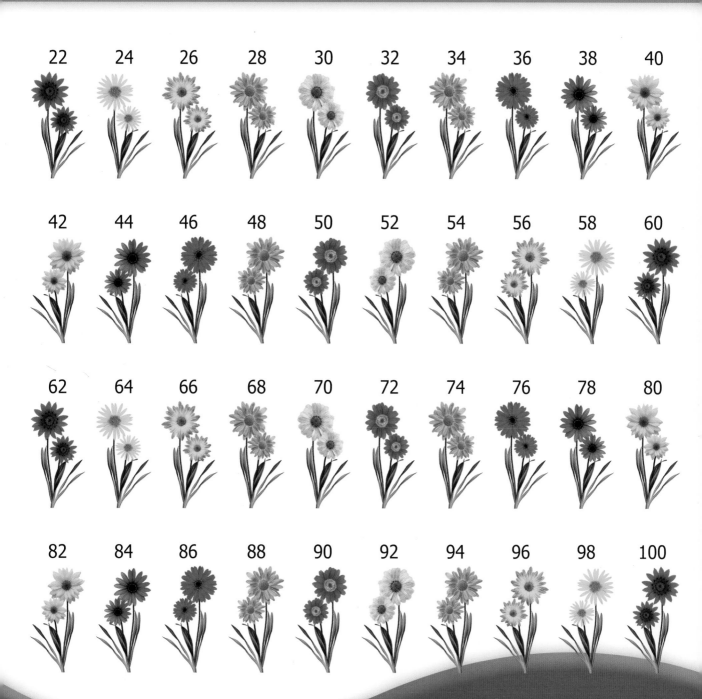

You can count to 100 by 5's.
Let's count!

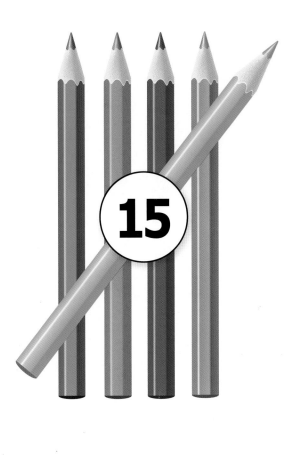

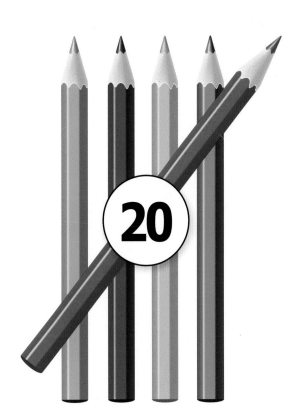

Keep counting!

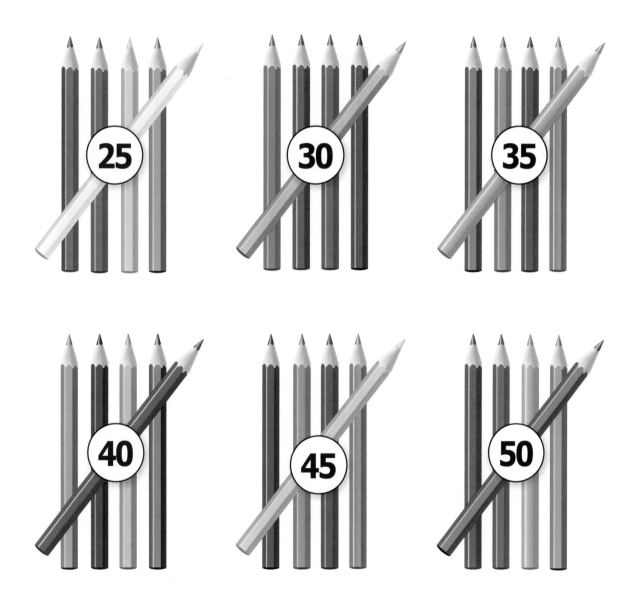

Don't stop!

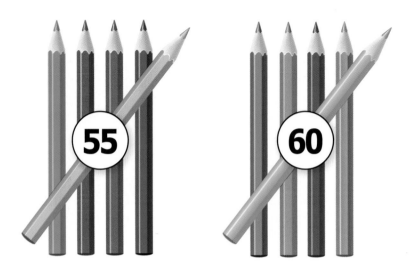

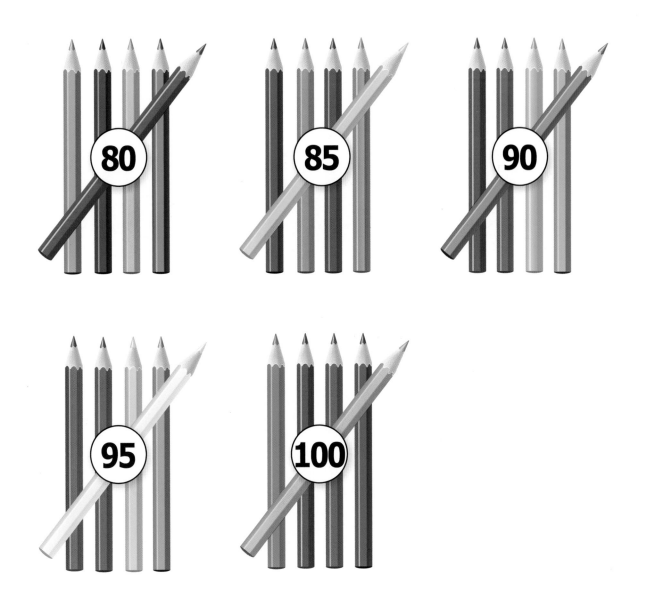

You can count to 100 by 10's.
Let's count!

= 10

= 20

= 30

= 40

= 50

$= 60$

$= 70$

$= 80$

$= 90$

$= 100$

There are many ways to count to 100!

By **1's**

By **2's**

By **5's**

By **10's**

Index

1's   4, 22
2's   8, 22
5's   12, 23
10's   18, 23

Websites

www.abcya.com/connect_the_dots_1-100.htm

teacher.scholastic.com/max/coins/index.htm

www.aaamath.com/g14c-nextnum-100.html

About the Author

Any way you count it, Joanne Mattern has written more than 300 books. Joanne lives in New York State with her husband, four children, and an assortment of pets that includes a dog, cats, reptiles, and fish.